WARRING
WITH
THE
SCRIPTURES

McDougal & Associates

Servants of Christ and Stewards of the
Mysteries of God

WARRING

WITH

THE

SCRIPTURES

Arm Yourself with Power-
Packed Words to Reign in Victory

by

Prophetess Jackie Harewood

Unless otherwise noted, all Scripture quotations are from *The Holy Bible, Authorized King James Version,* public domain. References marked GW are from *GOD'S WORD*, copyright © 1995 by God's Word to the Nations. References marked NIV are from the *Holy Bible, New International Version,* copyright © 1973, 1978, 1984 by International Bible Society, Colorado Springs, Colorado. References marked BSB are from the Berean Study Bible © 2016 by Bible Hub and Berean Bible. References marked GNT are from the *Good News Translation of the Bible*, copyright © 1992 by American Bible Society.

Published by:

McDougal & Associates
18896 Greenwell Springs RD
Greenwell Springs, LA 70739
www.thepublishedword.com

McDougal & Associates is dedicated to the spreading of the Gospel of Jesus Christ to as many people as possible in the shortest time possible.

ISBN 978-1-940461-73-1

Printed in the US, the UK and Australia
For Worldwide Distribution

DEDICATION

I dedicate this book to Mrs. Gladys Pryor Young, my mom. Thank you for what you have instilled in me. You are now resting with Jesus, and for that, I am grateful.

I love you.

ACKNOWLEDGEMENTS

I'd like to thank my mother for giving me the inspiration to pursue the fullness of God. "Auntie Gladys" to some, "Mother Gladys" to others, and "Mom" to me, she was known and loved by many. Throughout her illness we sat together as I worked on my computer to complete this book. She was always encouraging me to stay the course. She has since transitioned to Heaven and didn't get a chance to see the final product, but I know she is pleased with my work.

Thank you, Mom, for loving me and trusting me to express my gifts.

For the word of God is living and active, and sharper than any two-edged sword, penetrating even as far as the division of soul and spirit, and of joints and marrows, and able to judge the thoughts and intentions of the heart.

Hebrews 4:12, BSB

CONTENTS

Hebrews 4:12

For the word of God IS quick, and powerful, and sharper *than any two-edged sword, piercing even to the dividing asunder of soul and spirit, and of the joints and marrow, and is a discerner of the thoughts and intents of the heart.*

INTRODUCTION

There are many different forms of intercessory prayer, but none of them is more powerful than taking God's own words as they are recorded in the sacred Scriptures and turning them against the enemy. In this way, we are actually *Warring with the Scriptures*.

Jesus is our example, and He used the Word of God in this way. In His darkest hour, when the enemy had come against Him with all of his force (intent on destroying Him before He could even begin His ministry), Jesus refused to use any earthly means of defense.

Instead, He turned to His Father's own words and answered back, *"It is written ... ,* and it worked. Jesus was able to resist the enemy's advances and go on to fulfill His calling here on earth. That's how powerful God's words are.

Today, you and I are blessed to have at our disposal this powerful tool—the Word of God in written form in our own language. In the pages that follow I present selected passages from the Scriptures that can be used to fight the enemy when he comes against you. Learn to use them well. Start *Warring with the Scriptures,* and you, too, will be victorious.

Prophetess Jackie Harewood
Baton Rouge, Louisiana

One

POWER WORDS ABOUT FAITH

Proverbs 3:5

*Trust in the L*ORD *with all thine heart; and lean not unto thine own understanding.*

Ephesians 2:8

For by grace are ye saved through faith; and that not of yourselves: it is the gift of God.

2 Corinthians 5:7

(For we walk by faith, not by sight.)

Hebrews 11:6

But without faith it is impossible to please him: for he that cometh to God must believe that he is, and that he is a rewarder of them that diligently seek him.

1 John 5:4

For whatsoever is born of God overcometh the world: and this is the victory that overcometh the world, even our faith.

Mark 9:23

Jesus said unto him, If thou canst believe, all things are possible to him that believeth.

Luke 17:6

And the Lord said, If ye had faith as a

grain of mustard seed, ye might say unto this sycamine tree, Be thou plucked up by the root, and be thou planted in the sea; and it should obey you.

Matthew 9:22

But Jesus turned him about, and when he saw her, he said, Daughter, be of good comfort; thy faith hath made thee whole. And the woman was made whole from that hour.

1 John 5:14

And this is the confidence that we have in him, that, if we ask any thing according to his will, he heareth us.

Philippians 4:13

I can do all things through Christ which strengtheneth me.

Ephesians 2:8-9

For by grace are ye saved through faith; and that not of yourselves: it is the gift of God.

Hebrews 11:1

Now faith is the substance of things hoped for, the evidence of things not seen.

Psalm 40:4

Blessed is that man that maketh the Lord *his trust, and respecteth not the proud, nor such as turn aside to lies.*

James 1:3

Knowing this, that the trying of your faith worketh patience.

Luke 7:50

And he said to the woman, Thy faith hath saved thee; go in peace.

Mark 11:23

For verily I say unto you, That whosoever shall say unto this mountain, Be thou removed, and be thou cast into the sea; and shall not doubt in his heart, but shall believe that those things which he saith shall come to pass; he shall have whatsoever he saith.

Matthew 9:29

Then touched he their eyes, saying, According to your faith be it unto you.

Mark 9:24

And straightway the father of the child

cried out, and said with tears, Lord, I believe; help thou mine unbelief.

James 2:24

Ye see then how that by works a man is justified, and not by faith only.

Hebrews 13:5

Let your conversation be without covetousness; and be content with such things as ye have: for he hath said, I will never leave thee, nor forsake thee.

John 3:36

He that believeth on the Son hath everlasting life: and he that believeth not the Son shall not see life; but the wrath of God abideth on him.

1 Timothy 4:10

For therefore we both labour and suffer reproach, because we trust in the living God, who is the Saviour of all men, specially of those that believe.

Mark 11:22-24

And Jesus answering saith unto them, Have faith in God. For verily I say unto you, That whosoever shall say unto this mountain, Be thou removed, and be thou cast into the sea; and shall not doubt in his heart, but shall believe that those things which he saith shall come to pass; he shall have whatsoever he saith.

Therefore I say unto you, What things soever ye desire, when ye pray, believe that ye receive them, and ye shall have them.

Acts 26:18

To open their eyes, and to turn them from darkness to light, and from the power of Satan unto God, that they may receive forgiveness of sins, and inheritance among them which are sanctified by faith that is in me.

Mark 5:25-34

And a certain woman, which had an issue of blood twelve years, And had suffered many things of many physicians, and had spent all that she had, and was nothing bettered, but rather grew worse.

When she had heard of Jesus, came in the press behind, and touched his garment. For she said, If I may touch but his clothes, I shall be whole. And straightway the fountain of her blood was dried up; and she felt in her body that she was healed of that plague.

And Jesus, immediately knowing in himself that virtue had gone out of him, turned him about in the press, and said, Who touched my clothes?

And his disciples said unto him, Thou seest the multitude thronging thee, and sayest thou, Who touched me? And he looked round about to see her that had done this thing

But the woman fearing and trembling, knowing what was done in her, came and fell down before him, and told him all the truth. And he said unto her, Daughter, thy faith hath made thee whole; go in peace, and be whole of thy plague.

Hebrews 13:6

So that we may boldly say, The Lord is my helper, and I will not fear what man shall do unto me.

2 Timothy 1:12

For the which cause I also suffer these things: nevertheless I am not ashamed: for I know whom I have believed, and am persuaded that he is able to keep that which I have committed unto him against that day.

Acts 3:16

And his name through faith in his name hath made this man strong, whom ye see and know: yea, the faith which is by him hath given him this perfect soundness in the presence of you all.

James 1:12

Blessed is the man that endureth temptation: for when he is tried, he shall receive the crown of life, which the Lord hath promised to them that love him.

1 Peter 1:7

That the trial of your faith, being much more precious than of gold that perisheth, though it be tried with fire, might be found unto praise and honour and glory at the appearing of Jesus Christ.

Ephesians 6:16

Above all, taking the shield of faith, wherewith ye shall be able to quench all the fiery darts of the wicked.

Galatians 5:22

But the fruit of the Spirit is love, joy,

peace, longsuffering, gentleness, good-ness, faith.

Romans 8:28

And we know that all things work to-gether for good to them that love God, to them who are the called according to his purpose.

Matthew 8:2

And, behold, there came a leper and worshipped him, saying, Lord, if thou wilt, thou canst make me clean.

1 Corinthians 2:5

That your faith should not stand in the wisdom of men, but in the power of God.

John 6:69

And we believe and are sure that thou

art that Christ, the Son of the living God.

John 3:16

For God so loved the world, that he gave his only begotten Son, that whoso-ever believeth in him should not perish, but have everlasting life.

Psalm 18:6

In my distress I called upon the Lord, and cried unto my God: he heard my voice out of his temple, and my cry came before him, even into his ears.

Romans 15:13

Now the God of hope fill you with all joy and peace in believing, that ye may abound in hope, through the power of the Holy Ghost.

Luke 5:5

And Simon answering said unto him, Master, we have toiled all the night, and have taken nothing: nevertheless at thy word I will let down the net.

Matthew 9:21

For she said within herself, If I may but touch his garment, I shall be whole.

Isaiah 40:31

*But they that wait upon the L*ORD *shall renew their strength; they shall mount up with wings as eagles; they shall run, and not be weary; and they shall walk, and not faint.*

Matthew 9:18

While he spake these things unto them, behold, there came a certain ruler, and worshipped him, saying, My daughter is even now dead: but come and lay thy hand upon her, and she shall live.

1 Samuel 14:6

And Jonathan said to the young man that bare his armour, Come, and let us go over unto the garrison of these uncircumcised: it may be that the LORD will work for us: for there is no restraint to the LORD to save by many or by few.

Galatians 3:1-29

O foolish Galatians, who hath be-witched you, that ye should not obey the truth, before whose eyes Jesus Christ hath been evidently set forth, crucified among you? This only would I learn of you, Received ye the Spirit by the works of the law, or by the hearing of faith?

Are ye so foolish? Having begun in the Spirit, are ye now made perfect by the flesh? Have ye suffered so many things in vain? if it be yet in vain.

He therefore that ministereth to you the Spirit, and worketh miracles among you, doeth he it by the works of the law, or by the hearing of faith? Even as Abraham believed God, and it was accounted to him for righteousness. Know ye therefore that they which are of faith, the same are the children of Abraham. And the scripture, foreseeing that God would justify the heathen through faith, preached before the gospel unto Abraham, saying, In thee shall all nations be blessed.

So then they which be of faith are blessed with faithful Abraham. For as many as are of the works of the law are under the curse: for it is written, Cursed is every one that continueth not in all things which are written in the book of the law to do them. But that no man is justified by the law in the sight of God, it is evident: for, the just shall live by faith. And the law is not of faith: but, The man that doeth them shall live in them.

Christ hath redeemed us from the curse of the law, being made a curse for us: for it is written, Cursed is every one that hangeth on a tree: that the blessing of Abraham might come on the Gentiles through Jesus Christ; that we might receive the promise of the Spirit through faith.

Brethren, I speak after the manner of men; though it be but a man's covenant, yet if it be confirmed, no man disannulleth, or addeth thereto. Now to Abraham and his seed were the promises made. He saith not, And to seeds, as of many; but as of one, And to thy seed, which is Christ.

And this I say, that the covenant, that was confirmed before of God in Christ, the law, which was four hundred and thirty years after, cannot disannul, that it should make the promise of none effect. For if the inheritance be of the law, it is no more of promise: but God gave it to Abraham by promise.

Wherefore then serveth the law? It was added because of transgressions, till the seed should come to whom the promise was made; and it was ordained by angels in the hand of a mediator. Now a mediator is not a mediator of one, but God is one.

Is the law then against the promises of God? God forbid: for if there had been a law given which could have given life, verily righteousness should have been by the law. But the scripture hath concluded all under sin, that the promise by faith of Jesus Christ might be given to them that believe. But before faith came, we were kept under the law, shut up unto the faith which should afterwards be revealed.

Wherefore the law was our schoolmaster to bring us unto Christ, that we might be justified by faith. But after that faith is come, we are no longer under a schoolmaster. For ye are all the children of God by faith in Christ Jesus. For as many of you as have been baptized into Christ have put on Christ. There is neither Jew nor Greek, there is neither bond nor free, there is neither male nor female: for ye are all one in Christ Jesus. And if ye be Christ's, then are ye Abraham's seed, and heirs according to the promise.

Romans 3:22-28

Even the righteousness of God which is by faith of Jesus Christ unto all and upon all them that believe: for there is no difference: for all have sinned, and come short of the glory of God; Being justified freely by his grace through the redemption that is in Christ Jesus: Whom God hath set forth to be a propitiation through faith in his blood, to declare his righteousness for the remission of sins that are past, through the forbearance of God.

To declare, I say, at this time his righteousness: that he might be just, and the justifier of him which believeth in Jesus. Where is boasting then? It is excluded. By what law? of works? Nay: but by the law of faith. Therefore we conclude that a man is justified by faith without the deeds of the law.

John 6:68

Then Simon Peter answered him, Lord, to whom shall we go? thou hast the words of eternal life.

Habakkuk 2:4

Behold, his soul which is lifted up is not upright in him: but the just shall live by his faith.

Isaiah 55:11

So shall my word be that goeth forth out of my mouth: it shall not return unto me void, but it shall accomplish that which I please, and it shall prosper in the thing whereto I sent it.

Hebrews 11:4

By faith Abel offered unto God a more excellent sacrifice than Cain, by which he obtained witness that he was righteous, God testifying of his gifts: and by it he being dead yet speaketh.

Ephesians 6:10-13

Finally, my brethren, be strong in the Lord, and in the power of his might. Put on the whole armour of God, that ye may be able to stand against the wiles of the devil. For we wrestle not against flesh and blood, but against principalities, against powers, against the rulers of the darkness of this world, against spiritual wickedness in high places. Wherefore take unto you the whole armour of God, that ye may be able to withstand in the evil day, and having done all, to stand.

John 20:31

But these are written, that ye might believe that Jesus is the Christ, the Son of God; and that believing ye might have life through his name.

Matthew 17:20

And Jesus said unto them, Because of your unbelief: for verily I say unto you, If ye have faith as a grain of mustard seed, ye shall say unto this mountain, Remove hence to yonder place; and it shall remove; and nothing shall be impossible unto you.

Genesis 50:20

But as for you, ye thought evil against me; but God meant it unto good, to bring to pass, as it is this day, to save much people alive.

Hebrews 6:13-15

For when God made promise to Abraham, because he could swear by no greater, he sware by himself, Saying, Surely blessing I will bless thee, and multiplying I will multiply thee. And so, after he had patiently endured, he obtained the promise.

Colossians 2:7

Rooted and built up in him, and stablished in the faith, as ye have been taught, abounding therein with thanksgiving.

Philippians 1:27

Only let your conversation be as it becometh the gospel of Christ: that whether I come and see you, or else be absent, I may hear of your affairs, that ye stand fast in one spirit, with one mind striving together for the faith of the gospel.

1 Samuel 17:37

David said moreover, The LORD that delivered me out of the paw of the lion, and out of the paw of the bear, he will deliver me out of the hand of this

Philistine. And Saul said unto David, Go, and the LORD be with thee.

Revelation 3:20

Behold, I stand at the door, and knock: if any man hear my voice, and open the door, I will come in to him, and will sup with him, and he with me.

Revelation 2:19

I know thy works, and charity, and service, and faith, and thy patience, and thy works; and the last to be more than the first.

Hebrews 11:24-28

By faith Moses, when he was come to years, refused to be called the son of Pharaoh's daughter; choosing rather to suffer affliction with the people of God, than to enjoy the pleasures of sin for a season; esteeming the reproach of Christ greater riches than the treasures in Egypt: for he had respect unto the recompence of the reward. By faith he forsook Egypt, not fearing the wrath of the king: for he endured, as seeing him who is invisible. Through faith he kept the passover, and the sprinkling of blood, lest he that destroyed the first-born should touch them.

Hebrews 10:39

But we are not of them who draw back unto perdition; but of them that believe to the saving of the soul.

Hebrews 10:35

Cast not away therefore your confidence, which hath great recompence of reward.

Galatians 2:16

Knowing that a man is not justified by the works of the law, but by the faith of Jesus Christ, even we have believed in Jesus Christ, that we might be justified by the faith of Christ, and not by the works of the law: for by the works of the law shall no flesh be justified.

Romans 8:39

Nor height, nor depth, nor any other creature, shall be able to separate us from the love of God, which is in Christ Jesus our Lord.

Romans 8:37

Nay, in all these things we are more than conquerors through him that loved us.

Romans 8:35

Who shall separate us from the love of Christ? shall tribulation, or distress, or persecution, or famine, or nakedness, or peril, or sword?

Psalm 7:1

O Lord my God, in thee do I put my trust: save me from all them that persecute me, and deliver me.

2 Kings 18:5

He trusted in the Lord God of Israel; so that after him was none like him among all the kings of Judah, nor any that were before him.

2 Peter 3:13

Nevertheless we, according to his promise, look for new heavens

41

and a new earth, wherein dwelleth righteousness.

James 1:6

But let him ask in faith, nothing wavering. For he that wavereth is like a wave of the sea driven with the wind and tossed.

Hebrews 13:7

Remember them which have the rule over you, who have spoken unto you the word of God: whose faith follow, considering the end of their conversation.

Hebrews 11:7

By faith Noah, being warned of God of things not seen as yet, moved with fear, prepared an ark to the saving of his house; by the which he condemned the world, and became heir of the righteousness which is by faith.

Hebrews 10:38

Now the just shall live by faith: but if any man draw back, my soul shall have no pleasure in him.

Hebrews 6:12

That ye be not slothful, but followers of them who through faith and patience inherit the promises.

2 Timothy 4:7

I have fought a good fight, I have finished my course, I have kept the faith.

1 Timothy 1:19

Holding faith, and a good conscience;

which some having put away con-cerning faith have made shipwreck.

2 Thessalonians 1:3-5

We are bound to thank God always for you, brethren, as it is meet, because that your faith groweth exceedingly, and the charity of every one of you all toward each other aboundeth; So that we our-selves glory in you in the churches of God for your patience and faith in all your persecutions and tribulations that ye endure: Which is a manifest token of the righteous judgment of God that ye may be counted worthy of the kingdom of God, for which ye also suffer.

Romans 10:6-10

But the righteousness which is of faith speaketh on this wise, Say not in thine heart, Who shall ascend into heaven? (that is, to bring Christ down from above:) Or, Who shall descend into the deep? (that is, to bring up Christ again from the dead.) But what saith it? The word is nigh thee, even in thy mouth, and in thy heart: that is, the word of faith, which we preach; That if thou shalt confess with thy mouth the Lord Jesus, and shalt believe in thine heart that God hath raised him from the dead, thou shalt be saved. For with the heart man believeth unto righteousness; and with the mouth confession is made unto salvation.

Mark 16:16

He that believeth and is baptized shall be saved; but he that believeth not shall be damned.

Matthew 13:58

And he did not many mighty works there because of their unbelief.

Matthew 9:28

And when he was come into the house, the blind men came to him: and Jesus saith unto them, Believe ye that I am able to do this? They said unto him, Yea, Lord.

2 Chronicles 32:7

Be strong and courageous, be not afraid nor dismayed for the king of Assyria, nor for all the multitude that is with him: for there be more with us than with him.

Hebrews 12:2

Looking unto Jesus the author and

finisher of our faith; who for the joy that was set before him endured the cross, despising the shame, and is set down at the right hand of the throne of God.

Hebrews 11:32

And what shall I more say? for the time would fail me to tell of Gedeon, and of Barak, and of Samson, and of Jephthae; of David also, and Samuel, and of the prophets.

2 Timothy 2:11-13

It is a faithful saying: For if we be dead with him, we shall also live with him: If we suffer, we shall also reign with him: if we deny him, he also will deny us: If we believe not, yet he abideth faithful: he cannot deny himself.

2 Timothy 1:13

Hold fast the form of sound words, which thou hast heard of me, in faith and love which is in Christ Jesus.

1 Timothy 3:9

Holding the mystery of the faith in a pure conscience.

Colossians 1:23

If ye continue in the faith grounded and settled, and be not moved away from the hope of the gospel, which ye have heard, and which was preached to every creature which is under heaven; whereof I Paul am made a minister.

Galatians 5:6

For in Jesus Christ neither circumcision

availeth any thing, nor uncircumcision; but faith which worketh by love.

2 Corinthians 4:16-18

For which cause we faint not; but though our outward man perish, yet the inward man is renewed day by day. For our light affliction, which is but for a moment, worketh for us a far more exceeding and eternal weight of glory; While we look not at the things which are seen, but at the things which are not seen: for the things which are seen are temporal; but the things which are not seen are eternal.

Romans 10:17

So then faith cometh by hearing, and hearing by the word of God.

Romans 3:23

For all have sinned, and come short of the glory of God.

2 Chronicles 32:8

With him is an arm of flesh; but with us is the Lord our God to help us, and to fight our battles. And the people rested themselves upon the words of Hezekiah king of Judah.

Jude 1:21

Keep yourselves in the love of God, looking for the mercy of our Lord Jesus Christ unto eternal life.

1 Peter 1:21

Who by him do believe in God, that raised him up from the dead, and gave him glory; that your faith and hope might be in God.

1 Peter 1:8

Whom having not seen, ye love; in whom, though now ye see him not, yet believing, ye rejoice with joy unspeakable and full of glory.

Hebrews 11:23

By faith Moses, when he was born, was hid three months of his parents, because they saw he was a proper child; and they were not afraid of the king's commandment.

POWER WORDS ABOUT HEALING

Isaiah 41:10

Fear thou not; for I am with thee: be not dismayed; for I am thy God: I will strengthen thee; yea, I will help thee; yea, I will uphold thee with the right hand of my righteousness.

Jeremiah 17:14

Heal me, O LORD, and I shall be healed; save me, and I shall be saved: for thou art my praise.

1 Peter 2:24

Who his own self bare our sins in his own body on the tree, that we, being dead to sins, should live unto righteousness: by whose stripes ye were healed.

Isaiah 53:5

But he was wounded for our transgressions, he was bruised for our iniquities: the chastisement of our peace was upon him; and with his stripes we are healed.

Jeremiah 33:6

Behold, I will bring it health and cure, and I will cure them, and will reveal unto them the abundance of peace and truth.

Psalm 103:2-4

Bless the LORD, O my soul, and forget

not all his benefits: who forgiveth all thine iniquities; who healeth all thy diseases; who redeemeth thy life from destruction; who crowneth thee with lovingkindness and tender mercies.

James 5:14-15

Is any sick among you? let him call for the elders of the church; and let them pray over him, anointing him with oil in the name of the Lord: and the prayer of faith shall save the sick, and the Lord shall raise him up; and if he have committed sins, they shall be forgiven him.

Matthew 10:1

And when he had called unto him his twelve disciples, he gave them power against unclean spirits, to cast them out, and to heal all manner of sickness and all manner of disease.

James 5:16

Confess your faults one to another, and pray one for another, that ye may be healed. The effectual fervent prayer of a righteous man availeth much.

3 John 1:2

Beloved, I wish above all things that thou mayest prosper and be in health, even as thy soul prospereth.

Philippians 4:19

But my God shall supply all your need according to his riches in glory by Christ Jesus.

Matthew 10:8

Heal the sick, cleanse the lepers, raise the dead, cast out devils: freely ye have received, freely give.

Proverbs 17:22

A merry heart doeth good like a medicine: but a broken spirit drieth the bones.

Psalm 127:3

Lo, children are an heritage of the LORD: and the fruit of the womb is his reward.

Deuteronomy 7:15

And the LORD will take away from thee all sickness, and will put none of the evil diseases of Egypt, which thou knowest, upon thee; but will lay them upon all them that hate thee.

Romans 5:3-4

And not only so, but we glory in tribulations also: knowing that tribulation worketh patience; And patience, experience; and experience, hope.

Hebrews 11:6

But without faith it is impossible to please him: for he that cometh to God must believe that he is, and that he is a rewarder of them that diligently seek him.

Isaiah 54:17

No weapon that is formed against thee shall prosper; and every tongue that shall rise against thee in judgment thou shalt condemn. This is the heritage of the servants of the LORD, *and their righteousness is of me, saith the* LORD.

Proverbs 16:24

Pleasant words are as an honeycomb, sweet to the soul, and health to the bones.

Matthew 11:28

Come unto me, all ye that labour and are heavy laden, and I will give you rest.

Proverbs 4:20-22

My son, attend to my words; incline thine ear unto my sayings.

Let them not depart from thine eyes; keep them in the midst of thine heart.

For they are life unto those that find them, and health to all their flesh.

James 4:7

Submit yourselves therefore to God. Resist the devil, and he will flee from you.

Isaiah 57:18

I have seen his ways, and will heal him: I will lead him also, and restore comforts unto him and to his mourners.

Hebrews 11:1

Now faith is the substance of things hoped for, the evidence of things not seen.

2 Corinthians 12:9

And he said unto me, My grace is sufficient for thee: for my strength is made perfect in weakness. Most gladly therefore will I rather glory in my infirmities, that the power of Christ may rest upon me.

John 10:10

The thief cometh not, but for to steal, and to kill, and to destroy: I am come that they might have life, and that they might have it more abundantly.

Luke 4:18

The Spirit of the Lord is upon me, because he hath anointed me to preach the gospel to the poor; he hath sent me to heal the brokenhearted, to preach deliverance to the captives, and recovering of sight to the blind, to set at liberty them that are bruised.

Psalm 34:20

He keepeth all his bones: not one of them is broken.

Psalm 6:2

Have mercy upon me, O Lord; for I am weak: O Lord, heal me; for my bones are vexed.

Deuteronomy 32:39

See now that I, even I, am he, and there is no god with me: I kill, and I make alive; I wound, and I heal: neither is there any that can deliver out of my hand.

Hebrews 13:8

Jesus Christ the same yesterday, and to day, and for ever.

Romans 12:2

And be not conformed to this world: but be ye transformed by the renewing of your mind, that ye may prove what is that good, and acceptable, and perfect, will of God.

Romans 12:1-2

I beseech you therefore, brethren, by the mercies of God, that ye present your bodies a living sacrifice, holy, acceptable unto God, which is your reasonable service. And be not conformed to this world: but be ye transformed by the renewing of your mind, that ye may prove what is that good, and acceptable, and perfect, will of God.

Numbers 6:25-27

The LORD make his face shine upon

*thee, and be gracious unto thee: the
L<small>ORD</small> lift up his countenance upon
thee, and give thee peace. And they
shall put my name upon the children
of Israel; and I will bless them.*

1 Corinthians 11:17-32

*Now in this that I declare unto you I
praise you not, that ye come together
not for the better, but for the worse. For
first of all, when ye come together in the
church, I hear that there be divisions
among you; and I partly believe it. For
there must be also heresies among you,
that they which are approved may be
made manifest among you.*

*When ye come together therefore into
one place, this is not to eat the Lord's
supper. For in eating every one taketh
before other his own supper: and one*

is hungry, and another is drunken. What? have ye not houses to eat and to drink in? or despise ye the church of God, and shame them that have not? What shall I say to you? shall I praise you in this? I praise you not.

For I have received of the Lord that which also I delivered unto you, that the Lord Jesus the same night in which he was betrayed took bread: And when he had given thanks, he brake it, and said, Take, eat: this is my body, which is broken for you: this do in remembrance of me.

After the same manner also he took the cup, when he had supped, saying, This cup is the new testament in my blood: this do ye, as oft as ye drink it, in remembrance of me. For as often as ye eat this bread, and drink this cup, ye *do shew the Lord's death till he come. Wherefore whosoever shall eat this bread, and drink this cup of the Lord, unworthily, shall be guilty of the body and blood of the Lord. But let a man examine himself, and so let him eat of that bread, and drink of that cup. For he that eateth and drinketh unworthily, eateth and drinketh damnation to himself, not discerning the Lord's body. For this cause many are weak and sickly among you, and many sleep. For if we would judge ourselves, we should not be judged. But when we are judged, we are chastened of the Lord, that we should not be condemned with the world.*

Luke 10:9

And heal the sick that are therein, and

say unto them, The kingdom of God is come nigh unto you.

Matthew 9:27

And when Jesus departed thence, two blind men followed him, crying, and saying, Thou Son of David, have mercy on us.

Matthew 4:23

And Jesus went about all Galilee, teaching in their synagogues, and preaching the gospel of the kingdom, and healing all manner of sickness and all manner of disease among the people.

Jeremiah 30:17

For I will restore health unto thee, and I will heal thee of thy wounds, saith the LORD; because they called thee an

Outcast, saying, This is Zion, whom no man seeketh after.

Isaiah 57:18-19

I have seen his ways, and will heal him: I will lead him also, and restore comforts unto him and to his mourners. I create the fruit of the lips; Peace, peace to him that is far off, and to him that is near, saith the LORD; and I will heal him.

Psalm 51:1-19

Have mercy upon me, O God, according to thy lovingkindness: according unto the multitude of thy tender mercies blot out my transgressions. Wash me throughly from mine iniquity, and cleanse me from my sin. For I acknowledge my transgressions: and my sin is ever before me. Against thee, thee only, have I sinned, and done this evil in thy sight: that thou mightest be justified when thou speakest, and be clear when thou judgest.

Behold, I was shapen in iniquity; and in sin did my mother conceive me. Behold, thou desirest truth in the inward parts: and in the hidden part thou shalt make me to know wisdom. Purge me with hyssop, and I shall be clean: wash me, and I shall be whiter than snow. Make me to hear joy and gladness; that the bones which thou hast broken may rejoice. Hide thy face from my sins, and blot out all mine iniquities. Create in me a clean heart, O God; and renew a right spirit within me. Cast me not away from thy presence; and take not thy holy spirit from me.

Restore unto me the joy of thy salvation; and uphold me with thy free spirit. Then will I teach transgressors thy ways; and sinners shall be converted unto thee. Deliver me from bloodguiltiness, O God, thou God of my salvation: and my tongue shall sing aloud of thy righteousness. O Lord, open thou my lips; and my mouth shall shew forth thy praise. For thou desirest not sacrifice; else would I give it: thou delightest not in burnt offering. The sacrifices of God are a broken spirit: a broken and a contrite heart, O God, thou wilt not despise. Do good in thy good pleasure unto Zion: build thou the walls of Jerusalem. Then shalt thou be pleased with the sacrifices of righteousness, with burnt offering and whole burnt offering: then shall they offer bullocks upon thine altar.

Psalm 41:4

I said, LORD, be merciful unto me: heal my soul; for I have sinned against thee.

Numbers 12:13

And Moses cried unto the LORD, saying, Heal her now, O God, I beseech thee.

James 5:11

Behold, we count them happy which endure. Ye have heard of the patience of Job, and have seen the end of the Lord; that the Lord is very pitiful, and of tender mercy.

Acts 28:27

For the heart of this people is waxed gross, and their ears are dull of hearing, and their eyes have they closed;

lest they should see with their eyes, and hear with their ears, and understand with their heart, and should be converted, and I should heal them.

Acts 4:30

By stretching forth thine hand to heal; and that signs and wonders may be done by the name of thy holy child Jesus.

Acts 4:21-22

So when they had further threatened them, they let them go, finding nothing how they might punish them, because of the people: for all men glorified God for that which was done. For the man was above forty years old, on whom this miracle of healing was shewed.

Luke 5:17

And it came to pass on a certain day, as he was teaching, that there were Pharisees and doctors of the law sitting by, which were come out of every town of Galilee, and Judaea, and Jerusalem: and the power of the Lord was present to heal them.

Matthew 17:20

And Jesus said unto them, Because of your unbelief: for verily I say unto you, If ye have faith as a grain of mustard seed, ye shall say unto this mountain, Remove hence to yonder place; and it shall remove; and nothing shall be impossible unto you.

Matthew 13:15

For this people's heart is waxed gross,

and their ears are dull of hearing, and their eyes they have closed; lest at any time they should see with their eyes, and hear with their ears, and should understand with their heart, and should be converted, and I should heal them.

Ecclesiastes 3:1-3

To every thing there is a season, and a time to every purpose under the heaven: A time to be born, and a time to die; a time to plant, and a time to pluck up that which is planted; A time to kill, and a time to heal; a time to break down, and a time to build up.

Job 5:17-18

Behold, happy is the man whom God correcteth: therefore despise not thou the chastening of the Almighty: for he maketh sore, and bindeth up: he woundeth, and his hands make whole.

1 Peter 2:21-25

For even hereunto were ye called: because Christ also suffered for us, leaving us an example, that ye should follow his steps: who did no sin, neither was guile found in his mouth: who, when he was reviled, reviled not again; when he suffered, he threatened not; but committed himself to him that judgeth righteously: who his own self bare our sins in his own body on the tree, that we, being dead to sins, should live unto righteousness: by whose stripes ye were healed.

Ephesians 4:1-32

I therefore, the prisoner of the Lord, beseech you that ye walk worthy of the vocation wherewith ye are called, with all lowliness and meekness, with longsuffering, forbearing one another in love; endeavouring to keep the unity of the Spirit in the bond of peace. There is one body, and one Spirit, even as ye are called in one hope of your calling; one Lord, one faith, one baptism, one God and Father of all, who is above all, and through all, and in you all. But unto every one of us is given grace according to the measure of the gift of Christ.

Wherefore he saith, When he ascended up on high, he led captivity captive, and gave gifts unto men. (Now that he ascended, what is it but that he also descended first into the lower parts of the earth? He that descended is the same also that ascended up far above all heavens, that he might fill all things.)

And he gave some, apostles; and some, prophets; and some, evangelists; and some, pastors and teachers; for the perfecting of the saints, for the work of the ministry, for the edifying of the body of Christ: till we all come in the unity of the faith, and of the knowledge of the Son of God, unto a perfect man, unto the measure of the stature of the fulness of Christ.

That we henceforth be no more children, tossed to and fro, and carried about with every wind of doctrine, by the sleight of men, and cunning craftiness, whereby they lie in wait to *deceive; but speaking the truth in love, may grow up into him in all things, which is the head, even Christ: from whom the whole body fitly joined together and compacted by that which every joint supplieth, according to the effectual working in the measure of every part, maketh increase of the body unto the edifying of itself in love. This I say therefore, and testify in the Lord, that ye henceforth walk not as other Gentiles walk, in the vanity of their mind, having the understanding darkened, being alienated from the life of God through the ignorance that is in them, because of the blindness of their heart: who being past feeling have given themselves over unto lasciviousness, to work all uncleanness with greediness.*

But ye have not so learned Christ; if so be that ye have heard him, and have been taught by him, as the truth is in Jesus: that ye put off concerning the former conversation the old man, which is corrupt according to the deceitful lusts; and be renewed in the spirit of your mind; and that ye put on the new man, which after God is created in righteousness and true holiness.

Wherefore putting away lying, speak every man truth with his neighbour: for we are members one of another. Be ye angry, and sin not: let not the sun go down upon your wrath. Neither give place to the devil.

Let him that stole steal no more: but rather let him labour, working with his hands the thing which is good, that he may have to give to him that needeth.

Let no corrupt communication proceed out of your mouth, but that which is good to the use of edifying, that it may minister grace unto the hearers.

And grieve not the holy Spirit of God, whereby ye are sealed unto the day of redemption. Let all bitterness, and wrath, and anger, and clamour, and evil speaking, be put away from you, with all malice: and be ye kind one to another, tenderhearted, forgiving one another, even as God for Christ's sake hath forgiven you.

2 Corinthians 7:1

Having therefore these promises, dearly beloved, let us cleanse ourselves from all filthiness of the flesh and spirit, perfecting holiness in the fear of God.

2 Corinthians 5:7

(For we walk by faith, not by sight.)

2 Corinthians 1:3

Blessed be God, even the Father of our Lord Jesus Christ, the Father of mercies, and the God of all comfort.

1 Corinthians 12:9

To another faith by the same Spirit; to another the gifts of healing by the same Spirit.

Acts 10:38

How God anointed Jesus of Nazareth with the Holy Ghost and with power: who went about doing good, and healing all that were oppressed of the devil; for God was with him.

John 14:27

Peace I leave with you, my peace I give unto you: not as the world giveth, give I unto you. Let not your heart be troubled, neither let it be afraid.

John 12:40

He hath blinded their eyes, and hardened their heart; that they should not see with their eyes, nor understand with their heart, and be converted, and I should heal them.

Luke 7:7

Wherefore neither thought I myself worthy to come unto thee: but say in a word, and my servant shall be healed.

Mark 1:30-31

But Simon's wife's mother lay sick of

a fever, and anon they tell him of her. And he came and took her by the hand, and lifted her up; and immediately the fever left her, and she ministered unto them.

Isaiah 57:19

I create the fruit of the lips; Peace, peace to him that is far off, and to him that is near, saith the LORD; and I will heal him.

Isaiah 19:22

And the LORD shall smite Egypt: he shall smite and heal it: and they shall return even to the LORD, and he shall be intreated of them, and shall heal them.

Ecclesiastes 3:11

He hath made every thing beautiful in

his time: also he hath set the world in their heart, so that no man can find out the work that God maketh from the beginning to the end.

Psalm 119:77

Let thy tender mercies come unto me, that I may live: for thy law is my delight.

Psalm 119:71

It is good for me that I have been afflicted; that I might learn thy statutes.

Psalm 119:50

This is my comfort in my affliction: for thy word hath quickened me.

Psalm 119:40

Behold, I have longed after thy precepts: quicken me in thy righteousness.

Psalm 119:28

My soul melteth for heaviness: strengthen thou me according unto thy word.

Psalm 119:25

My soul cleaveth unto the dust: quicken thou me according to thy word.

Psalm 107:41

Yet setteth he the poor on high from affliction, and maketh him families like a flock.

Psalm 103:1-5

Bless the LORD, O my soul: and all that is within me, bless his holy name. Bless the LORD, O my soul, and forget not all his benefits: who forgiveth all thine iniquities; who healeth all thy diseases; who redeemeth thy life from destruction; who crowneth thee with lovingkindness and tender mercies; Who satisfieth thy mouth with good things; so that thy youth is renewed like the eagle's.

Psalm 41:3

The LORD will strengthen him upon the bed of languishing: thou wilt make all his bed in his sickness.

Psalm 41:1-3

Blessed is he that considereth the poor: the LORD will deliver him in time of trouble. The LORD will pre-serve him, and keep him alive; and he shall be blessed upon the earth: and thou wilt not deliver him unto the will of his enemies. The LORD will strengthen him upon the bed of languishing: thou wilt make all his bed in his sickness.

Psalm 35:27

Let them shout for joy, and be glad, that favour my righteous cause: yea, let them say continually, Let the Lord be magnified, which hath pleasure in the prosperity of his servant.

Psalm 34:6

This poor man cried, and the Lord heard him, and saved him out of all his troubles.

Job 5:26

Thou shalt come to thy grave in a full age, like as a shock of corn cometh in in his season.

2 Chronicles 7:14

If my people, which are called by my name, shall humble themselves, and pray, and seek my face, and turn from their wicked ways; then will I hear from heaven, and will forgive their sin, and will heal their land.

2 Kings 20:8-9

And Hezekiah said unto Isaiah, What shall be the sign that the LORD will heal me, and that I shall go up into the house of the LORD the third day? And Isaiah said, This sign shalt thou have of the LORD, that the LORD will do the thing that he hath spoken: shall the shadow go forward ten degrees, or go back ten degrees?

1 Samuel 12:16

Now therefore stand and see this great thing, which the LORD will do before your eyes.

Deuteronomy 32:36

For the LORD shall judge his people, and repent himself for his servants, when he seeth that their power is gone, and there is none shut up, or left.

Ephesians 2:2

Wherein in time past ye walked according to the course of this world, according to the prince of the power of the air, the spirit that now worketh in the children of disobedience.

Galatians 3:14

That the blessing of Abraham might

come on the Gentiles through Jesus Christ; that we might receive the promise of the Spirit through faith.

Romans 4:17

(As it is written, I have made thee a father of many nations,) before him whom he believed, even God, who quickeneth the dead, and calleth those things which be not as though they were.

Acts 4:16

Saying, What shall we do to these men? for that indeed a notable miracle hath been done by them is manifest to all them that dwell in Jerusalem; and we cannot deny it.

Acts 4:10

Be it known unto you all, and to all the people of Israel, that by the name of Jesus Christ of Nazareth, whom ye crucified, whom God raised from the dead, even by him doth this man stand here before you whole.

Acts 2:41-43

Then they that gladly received his word were baptized: and the same day there were added unto them about three thousand souls. And they continued stedfastly in the apostles' doctrine and fellowship, and in breaking of bread, and in prayers. And fear came upon every soul: and many wonders and signs were done by the apostles.

John 4:47

When he heard that Jesus was come out of Judaea into Galilee, he went unto him, and besought him that he would come down, and heal his son: for he was at the point of death.

Luke 14:4

And they held their peace. And he took him, and healed him, and let him go.

Luke 13:13

And he laid his hands on her: and immediately she was made straight, and glorified God.

Luke 13:12

And when Jesus saw her, he called her to him, and said unto her, Woman, thou art loosed from thine infirmity.

Luke 10:19-20

Behold, I give unto you power to tread on serpents and scorpions, and over all the power of the enemy: and nothing shall by any means hurt you. Notwithstanding in this rejoice not, that the spirits are subject unto you; but rather rejoice, because your names are written in heaven.

Luke 8:48

And he said unto her, Daughter, be of good comfort: thy faith hath made thee whole; go in peace.

THREE

POWER WORDS
ABOUT PEACE

Matthew 5:9

Blessed are the peacemakers: for they shall be called the children of God.

Philippians 4:7

And the peace of God, which passeth all understanding, shall keep your hearts and minds through Christ Jesus.

2 Thessalonians 3:16

Now the Lord of peace himself give you

peace always by all means. The Lord be with you all.

John 14:27

Peace I leave with you, my peace I give unto you: not as the world giveth, give I unto you. Let not your heart be troubled, neither let it be afraid.

1 Peter 3:11

Let him eschew evil, and do good; let him seek peace, and ensue it.

Philippians 4:6

Be careful for nothing; but in every thing by prayer and supplication with thanksgiving let your requests be made known unto God.

1 Peter 5:7

Casting all your care upon him; for he careth for you.

Romans 12:18

If it be possible, as much as lieth in you, live peaceably with all men.

Isaiah 26:3

Thou wilt keep him in perfect peace, whose mind is stayed on thee: because he trusteth in thee.

John 16:33

These things I have spoken unto you, that in me ye might have peace. In the world ye shall have tribulation: but be of good cheer; I have overcome the world.

Hebrews 12:14

Follow peace with all men, and holiness, without which no man shall see the Lord.

Philippians 4:9

Those things, which ye have both learned, and received, and heard, and seen in me, do: and the God of peace shall be with you.

Isaiah 12:2

Behold, God is my salvation; I will trust, and not be afraid: for the LORD JEHOVAH is my strength and my song; he also is become my salvation.

Romans 15:13

Now the God of hope fill you with all joy and peace in believing, that ye may abound in hope, through the power of the Holy Ghost.

Proverbs 12:20

Deceit is in the heart of them that imagine evil: but to the counsellors of peace is joy.

Romans 8:6

For to be carnally minded is death; but to be spiritually minded is life and peace.

1 Peter 3:9-11

Not rendering evil for evil, or railing for railing: but contrariwise blessing; knowing that ye are thereunto called, that ye should inherit a blessing.
For he that will love life, and see good days, let him refrain his tongue from

evil, and his lips that they speak no guile: let him eschew evil, and do good; let him seek peace, and ensue it.

James 2:14-24

What doth it profit, my brethren, though a man say he hath faith, and have not works? can faith save him? If a brother or sister be naked, and destitute of daily food, And one of you say unto them, Depart in peace, be ye warmed and filled; notwithstanding ye give them not those things which are needful to the body; what doth it profit? Even so faith, if it hath not works, is dead, being alone.

Yea, a man may say, Thou hast faith, and I have works: shew me thy faith without thy works, and I will shew thee my faith by my works. Thou believest that there is one God; thou doest well: the devils also believe, and tremble. But wilt thou know.

O vain man, that faith without works is dead? Was not Abraham our father justified by works, when he had offered Isaac his son upon the altar? Seest thou how faith wrought with his works, and by works was faith made perfect? And the scripture was fulfilled which saith, Abraham believed God, and it was imputed unto him for righteousness: and he was called the Friend of God. Ye see then how that by works a man is justified, and not by faith only.

1 Corinthians 14:33

For God is not the author of confusion, but of peace, as in all churches of the saints.

1 Peter 5:6-7

Humble yourselves therefore under the mighty hand of God, that he may exalt you in due time: Casting all your care upon him; for he careth for you.

Isaiah 54:10

For the mountains shall depart, and the hills be removed; but my kindness shall not depart from thee, neither shall the covenant of my peace be removed, saith the LORD that hath mercy on thee.

Philemon 1:3

Grace to you, and peace, from God our Father and the Lord Jesus Christ.

Romans 14:17

For the kingdom of God is not meat

and drink; but righteousness, and peace, and joy in the Holy Ghost.

Psalm 119:127

Therefore I love thy commandments above gold; yea, above fine gold.

1 Thessalonians 5:15

See that none render evil for evil unto any man; but ever follow that which is good, both among yourselves, and to all men.

Colossians 3:15

And let the peace of God rule in your hearts, to the which also ye are called in one body; and be ye thankful.

Galatians 5:22

But the fruit of the Spirit is love, joy,

peace, longsuffering, gentleness, good-
ness, faith.

Proverbs 16:7

When a man's ways please the Lord,
he maketh even his enemies to be at
peace with him.

Psalm 4:8

I will both lay me down in peace, and
sleep: for thou, Lord, *only makest me*
dwell in safety.

1 Peter 3:9

Not rendering evil for evil, or railing
for railing: but contrariwise blessing;
knowing that ye are thereunto called,
that ye should inherit a blessing.

James 3:18

And the fruit of righteousness is sown in peace of them that make peace.

1 Timothy 2:1-2

I exhort therefore, that, first of all, supplications, prayers, intercessions, and giving of thanks, be made for all men; for kings, and for all that are in authority; that we may lead a quiet and peaceable life in all godliness and honesty.

Romans 12:16-21

Be of the same mind one toward another. Mind not high things, but condescend to men of low estate. Be not wise in your own conceits. Recompense to no man evil for evil. Provide things honest in the sight of all men. If it be possible, as much as lieth in you, live peaceably with all men.

Dearly beloved, avenge not yourselves, but rather give place unto wrath: for it is written, Vengeance is mine; I will repay, saith the Lord. Therefore if thine enemy hunger, feed him; if he thirst, give him drink: for in so doing thou shalt heap coals of fire on his head. Be not overcome of evil, but overcome evil with good.

Ecclesiastes 4:6

Better is an handful with quietness, than both the hands full with travail and vexation of spirit.

Proverbs 17:1

Better is a dry morsel, and quietness therewith, than an house full of sacrifices with strife.

Leviticus 19:18

Thou shalt not avenge, nor bear any grudge against the children of thy people, but thou shalt love thy neighbour as thyself: I am the LORD.

Romans 14:19

Let us therefore follow after the things which make for peace, and things wherewith one may edify another.

Romans 12:17

Recompense to no man evil for evil. Provide things honest in the sight of all men.

Psalm 120:6

My soul hath long dwelt with him that hateth peace.

Luke 2:14

Glory to God in the highest, and on earth peace, good will toward men.

Psalm 37:4

Delight thyself also in the LORD; and he shall give thee the desires of thine heart.

Isaiah 32:17

And the work of righteousness shall be peace; and the effect of righteousness quietness and assurance for ever.

Proverbs 3:24

When thou liest down, thou shalt not be afraid: yea, thou shalt lie down, and thy sleep shall be sweet.

Romans 15:33

Now the God of peace be with you all. Amen.

John 7:38

He that believeth on me, as the scripture hath said, out of his belly shall flow rivers of living water.

Isaiah 54:13

And all thy children shall be taught of the LORD; and great shall be the peace of thy children.

Psalm 73:26

My flesh and my heart faileth: but God is the strength of my heart, and my portion for ever.

1 John 4:1

Beloved, believe not every spirit, but try the spirits whether they are of God: because many false prophets are gone out into the world.

1 Timothy 1:2

Unto Timothy, my own son in the faith: Grace, mercy, and peace, from God our Father and Jesus Christ our Lord.

Colossians 1:20

And, having made peace through the blood of his cross, by him to reconcile all things unto himself; by him, I say, whether they be things in earth, or things in heaven.

Galatians 3:28

There is neither Jew nor Greek, there is

neither bond nor free, there is neither male nor female: for ye are all one in Christ Jesus.

John 20:19

Then the same day at evening, being the first day of the week, when the doors were shut where the disciples were assembled for fear of the Jews, came Jesus and stood in the midst, and saith unto them, Peace be unto you.

Proverbs 3:13-18

Happy is the man that findeth wisdom, and the man that getteth understanding. For the merchandise of it is better than the merchandise of silver, and the gain thereof than fine gold. She is more precious than rubies: and all the things thou canst desire are not to be compared unto her. Length of days is in her right hand; and in her left hand riches and honour. Her ways are ways of pleasantness, and all her paths are peace. She is a tree of life to them that lay hold upon her: and happy is every one that retaineth her.

Psalm 34:14

Depart from evil, and do good; seek peace, and pursue it.

1 Peter 3:10

For he that will love life, and see good days, let him refrain his tongue from evil, and his lips that they speak no guile:

James 4:1-2

From whence come wars and fightings

among you? come they not hence, even of your lusts that war in your members? Ye lust, and have not: ye kill, and desire to have, and cannot obtain: ye fight and war, yet ye have not, because ye ask not.

James 1:8

A double minded man is unstable in all his ways.

Titus 1:4

To Titus, mine own son after the common faith: Grace, mercy, and peace, from God the Father and the Lord Jesus Christ our Saviour.

2 Timothy 1:2

To Timothy, my dearly beloved son: Grace, mercy, and peace, from God the Father and Christ Jesus our Lord.

Isaiah 57:2

He shall enter into peace: they shall rest in their beds, each one walking in his uprightness.

James 3:17

But the wisdom that is from above is first pure, then peaceable, gentle, and easy to be intreated, full of mercy and good fruits, without partiality, and without hypocrisy.

James 1:6-9

But let him ask in faith, nothing wavering. For he that wavereth is like a wave of the sea driven with the wind and tossed. For let not that man think that he shall receive any thing of the Lord.

A double minded man is unstable in all his ways. Let the brother of low degree rejoice in that he is exalted:

1 Timothy 5:8

But if any provide not for his own, and specially for those of his own house, he hath denied the faith, and is worse than an infidel.

1 Timothy 1:1-20

Paul, an apostle of Jesus Christ by the commandment of God our Saviour, and Lord Jesus Christ, which is our hope; unto Timothy, my own son in the faith: grace, mercy, and peace, from God our Father and Jesus Christ our Lord. As I besought thee to abide still at Ephesus, when I went into Macedonia, that thou mightest charge some that they teach no other doctrine, neither give heed to fables and endless genealogies, which minister questions, rather than godly edifying which is in faith: so do.

Now the end of the commandment is charity out of a pure heart, and of a good conscience, and of faith unfeigned: from which some having swerved have turned aside unto vain jangling; desiring to be teachers of the law; understanding neither what they say, nor whereof they affirm. But we know that the law is good, if a man use it lawfully; knowing this, that the law is not made for a righteous man, but for the lawless and disobedient, for the ungodly and for sinners, for unholy and profane, for murderers of fathers and murderers of mothers, for manslayers, for whoremongers, for them that defile themselves with mankind, for men-stealers, for liars, for perjured persons, and if there be any other thing that is contrary to sound doctrine; according to the glorious gospel of the blessed God, which was committed to my trust. And I thank Christ Jesus our Lord, who hath enabled me, for that he counted me faithful, putting me into the ministry; Who was before a blasphemer, and a persecutor, and injurious: but I obtained mercy, because I did it ignorantly in unbelief. And the grace of our Lord was exceeding abundant with faith and love which is in Christ Jesus. This is a faithful saying, and worthy of all acceptation, that Christ Jesus came into the world to save sinners; of whom I am chief. Howbeit for this cause I obtained mercy, that in me first Jesus Christ might shew forth all long-suffering, for a pattern to them which should hereafter believe on him to life everlasting.

Now unto the King eternal, immortal, invisible, the only wise God, be honour and glory for ever and ever. Amen.

This charge I commit unto thee, son Timothy, according to the prophecies which went before on thee, that thou by them mightest war a good warfare; holding faith, and a good conscience; which some having put away concerning faith have made shipwreck: of whom is Hymenaeus and Alexander; whom I have delivered unto Satan, that they may learn not to blaspheme.

Romans 5:1

Therefore being justified by faith, we have peace with God through our Lord Jesus Christ.

Mark 13:11

But when they shall lead you, and deliver you up, take no thought beforehand what ye shall speak, neither do ye premeditate: but whatsoever shall be given you in that hour, that speak ye: for it is not ye that speak, but the Holy Ghost.

Matthew 12:25

And Jesus knew their thoughts, and said unto them, Every kingdom divided against itself is brought to desolation; and every city or house divided against itself shall not stand.

Matthew 10:22

And ye shall be hated of all men for my name's sake: but he that endureth to the end shall be saved.

Matthew 6:34

Take therefore no thought for the morrow: for the morrow shall take thought for the things of itself. Sufficient unto the day is the evil thereof.

Matthew 6:31

Therefore take no thought, saying, What shall we eat? or, What shall we drink? or, Wherewithal shall we be clothed?

Matthew 6:25-34

Therefore I say unto you, Take no thought for your life, what ye shall eat, or what ye shall drink; nor yet for your body, what ye shall put on. Is not the life more than meat, and the body than raiment? Behold the fowls of the air: for they sow not, neither do they reap, nor gather into barns; yet your heavenly Father feedeth them. Are ye not much better than they?

Which of you by taking thought can add one cubit unto his stature? And why take ye thought for raiment? Consider the lilies of the field, how they grow; they toil not, neither do they spin: and yet I say unto you, That even Solomon in all his glory was not arrayed like one of these.

Wherefore, if God so clothe the grass of the field, which today is, and to morrow is cast into the oven, shall he not much more clothe you, O ye of little faith? Therefore take no thought, saying, What shall we eat? or, What shall we drink? or, Wherewithal shall we be clothed? (For after all these things do the Gentiles seek:) for your heavenly Father knoweth that ye have need of all these things.

But seek ye first the kingdom of God, and his righteousness; and all these things shall be added unto you. Take therefore no thought for the morrow: for the morrow shall take thought for the things of itself. Sufficient unto the day is the evil thereof.

Malachi 2:5

My covenant was with him of life and peace; and I gave them to him for the fear wherewith he feared me, and was afraid before my name.

Jeremiah 33:6

Behold, I will bring it health and cure, and I will cure them, and will reveal unto them the abundance of peace and truth.

Isaiah 55:12

For ye shall go out with joy, and be led forth with peace: the mountains and the hills shall break forth before you into singing, and all the trees of the field shall clap their hands.

Isaiah 53:4-5

Surely he hath borne our griefs, and carried our sorrows: yet we did esteem him stricken, smitten of God, and afflicted. But he was wounded for our transgressions, he was bruised for our iniquities: the chastisement of our peace was upon him; and with his stripes we are healed.

Isaiah 48:18

O that thou hadst hearkened to my commandments! then had thy peace been as a river, and thy righteousness as the waves of the sea:

Isaiah 41:10

Fear thou not; for I am with thee: be not dismayed; for I am thy God: I will strengthen thee; yea, I will help thee; yea, I will uphold thee with the right hand of my righteousness.

Isaiah 9:2-6

The people that walked in darkness have seen a great light: they that dwell in the land of the shadow of death, upon them hath the light shined. Thou hast multiplied the nation, and not increased the joy: they joy before thee according to the joy in harvest, and as men rejoice when they divide the spoil. For thou hast broken the yoke of his burden, and the staff of his shoulder, the rod of his oppressor, as in the day of Midian. For every battle of the warrior is with confused noise, and garments rolled in blood; but this shall be with burning and fuel of fire.

For unto us a child is born, unto us a son is given: and the government shall be upon his shoulder: and his name shall be called Wonderful, Counsellor, The mighty God, The everlasting Father, The Prince of Peace.

Proverbs 20:3

It is an honour for a man to cease from strife: but every fool will be meddling.

Job 5:23

For thou shalt be in league with the stones of the field: and the beasts of the field shall be at peace with thee.

James 2:14

What doth it profit, my brethren, though a man say he hath faith, and have not works? can faith save him?

Hebrews 12:4

Ye have not yet resisted unto blood, striving against sin.

Hebrews 2:11

For both he that sanctifieth and they

who are sanctified are all of one: for which cause he is not ashamed to call them brethren,

2 Corinthians 7:1

Having therefore these promises, dearly beloved, let us cleanse ourselves from all filthiness of the flesh and spirit, perfecting holiness in the fear of God.

Romans 13:4

For he is the minister of God to thee for good. But if thou do that which is evil, be afraid; for he beareth not the sword in vain: for he is the minister of God, a revenger to execute wrath upon him that doeth evil.

John 3:16

For God so loved the world, that he

*gave his only begotten Son, that whoso-
ever believeth in him should not perish,
but have everlasting life.*

Matthew 10:19

*But when they deliver you up, take no
thought how or what ye shall speak: for
it shall be given you in that same hour
what ye shall speak.*

Haggai 2:9

*The glory of this latter house shall be
greater than of the former, saith the
Lord of hosts: and in this place will I
give peace, saith the Lord of hosts.*

Isaiah 60:20

*Thy sun shall no more go down; neither
shall thy moon withdraw itself: for the
Lord shall be thine everlasting light,*

and the days of thy mourning shall be ended.

Isaiah 53:5

But he was wounded for our transgressions, he was bruised for our iniquities: the chastisement of our peace was upon him; and with his stripes we are healed.

Isaiah 32:18

And my people shall dwell in a peaceable habitation, and in sure dwellings, and in quiet resting places;

Isaiah 11:13

The envy also of Ephraim shall depart, and the adversaries of Judah shall be cut off: Ephraim shall not envy Judah, and Judah shall not vex Ephraim.

Isaiah 2:4

And he shall judge among the nations, and shall rebuke many people: and they shall beat their swords into plowshares, and their spears into pruninghooks: nation shall not lift up sword against nation, neither shall they learn war any more.

Proverbs 17:14

The beginning of strife is as when one letteth out water: therefore leave off contention, before it be meddled with.

Proverbs 15:17

Better is a dinner of herbs where love is, than a stalled ox and hatred therewith.

Psalm 103:1-5

Bless the LORD, O my soul: and all

that is within me, bless his holy name. Bless the LORD, O my soul, and forget not all his benefits: who forgiveth all thine iniquities; who healeth all thy diseases; who redeemeth thy life from destruction; who crowneth thee with lovingkindness and tender mercies; who satisfieth thy mouth with good things; so that thy youth is renewed like the eagle's.

Psalm 73:25

Whom have I in heaven but thee? and there is none upon earth that I desire beside thee.

Psalm 17:15

As for me, I will behold thy face in righteousness: I shall be satisfied, when I awake, with thy likeness.

Esther 10:3

For Mordecai the Jew was next unto king Ahasuerus, and great among the Jews, and accepted of the multitude of his brethren, seeking the wealth of his people, and speaking peace to all his seed.

Genesis 32:24

And Jacob was left alone; and there wrestled a man with him until the breaking of the day.

POWER WORDS ABOUT FORGIVENESS

Ephesians 4:32

And be ye kind one to another, tender-hearted, forgiving one another, even as God for Christ's sake hath forgiven you.

Mark 11:25

And when ye stand praying, forgive, if ye have ought against any: that your Father also which is in heaven may forgive you your trespasses.

1 Corinthians 10:13

There hath no temptation taken you but such as is common to man: but God is faithful, who will not suffer you to be tempted above that ye are able; but will with the temptation also make a way to escape, that ye may be able to bear it.

1 John 1:9

If we confess our sins, he is faithful and just to forgive us our sins, and to cleanse us from all unrighteousness. Romans 3:23
For all have sinned, and come short of the glory of God.

James 5:16

Confess your faults one to another, and pray one for another, that ye may be healed. The effectual fervent prayer of a righteous man availeth much.

James 2:8

If ye fulfil the royal law according to the scripture, Thou shalt love thy neighbour as thyself, ye do well.

Acts 22:16

And now why tarriest thou? arise, and be baptized, and wash away thy sins, calling on the name of the Lord.

Acts 10:43

To him give all the prophets witness, that through his name whosoever believeth in him shall receive remission of sins.

Acts 2:38

Then Peter said unto them, Repent, and be baptized every one of you in the name of Jesus Christ for the remission of sins, and ye shall receive the gift of the Holy Ghost.

Acts 2:14-47

But Peter, standing up with the eleven, lifted up his voice, and said unto them, Ye men of Judaea, and all ye that dwell at Jerusalem, be this known unto you, and hearken to my words.

Matthew 18:21-22

Then came Peter to him, and said, Lord, how oft shall my brother sin against me, and I forgive him? till seven times? Jesus saith unto him, I say not unto thee, Until seven times: but, Until seventy times seven.

Matthew 6:15-16

But if ye forgive not men their trespasses, neither will your Father forgive your trespasses. Moreover when ye fast, be not, as the hypocrites, of a sad countenance: for they disfigure their faces, that they may appear unto men to fast. Verily I say unto you, They have their reward.

1 John 1:8

If we say that we have no sin, we deceive ourselves, and the truth is not in us.

Romans 6:23

For the wages of sin is death; but the

gift of God is eternal life through Jesus Christ our Lord.

Romans 6:4

Therefore we are buried with him by baptism into death: that like as Christ was raised up from the dead by the glory of the Father, even so we also should walk in newness of life.

John 13:34

A new commandment I give unto you, That ye love one another; as I have loved you, that ye also love one another.

John 3:16

For God so loved the world, that he gave his only begotten Son, that whosoever believeth in him should not perish, but have everlasting life.

Matthew 26:28

For this is my blood of the new testament, which is shed for many for the remission of sins.

Matthew 7:21-22

Not every one that saith unto me, Lord, Lord, shall enter into the kingdom of heaven; but he that doeth the will of my Father which is in heaven.

Many will say to me in that day, Lord, Lord, have we not prophesied in thy name? and in thy name have cast out devils? and in thy name done many wonderful works?

Matthew 6:24

No man can serve two masters: for either he will hate the one, and love the other; or else he will hold to the one, and despise the other. Ye cannot serve God and mammon.

Matthew 6:12

And forgive us our debts, as we forgive our debtors.

Galatians 3:27

For as many of you as have been baptized into Christ have put on Christ.

2 Corinthians 7:1

Having therefore these promises, dearly beloved, let us cleanse ourselves from all filthiness of the flesh and spirit, perfecting holiness in the fear of God.

2 Corinthians 5:17

Therefore if any man be in Christ,

he is a new creature: old things are passed away; behold, all things are become new.

Five

POWER WORDS ABOUT TRUST

Proverbs 3:5

Trust in the LORD with all thine heart; and lean not unto thine own understanding.

1 John 4:18

There is no fear in love; but perfect love casteth out fear: because fear hath torment. He that feareth is not made perfect in love.

Jeremiah 29:11

For I know the thoughts that I think toward you, saith the LORD, thoughts of peace, and not of evil, to give you an expected end.

Psalm 56:2-4

What time I am afraid, I will trust in thee. In God I will praise his word, in God I have put my trust; I will not fear what flesh can do unto me.

Proverbs 3:1-6

My son, forget not my law; but let thine heart keep my commandments: For length of days, and long life, and peace, shall they add to thee.

Let not mercy and truth forsake thee: bind them about thy neck; write them upon the table of thine heart: so shalt thou find favour and good understanding in the sight of God and man.

Trust in the LORD *with all thine heart; and lean not unto thine own understanding. In all thy ways acknowledge him, and he shall direct thy paths.*

Psalm 13:5

But I have trusted in thy mercy; my heart shall rejoice in thy salvation.

Romans 10:9

That if thou shalt confess with thy mouth the Lord Jesus, and shalt believe in thine heart that God hath raised him from the dead, thou shalt be saved.

Jeremiah 29:10-14

For thus saith the LORD, *That after seventy years be accomplished at Babylon*

I will visit you, and perform my good word toward you, in causing you to return to this place.

For I know the thoughts that I think toward you, saith the LORD, thoughts of peace, and not of evil, to give you an expected end. Then shall ye call upon me, and ye shall go and pray unto me, and I will hearken unto you. And ye shall seek me, and find me, when ye shall search for me with all your heart. And I will be found of you, saith the LORD: and I will turn away your captivity, and I will gather you from all the nations, and from all the places whither I have driven you, saith the LORD; and I will bring you again into the place whence I caused you to be carried away captive.

Psalm 40:4

Blessed is that man that maketh the LORD *his trust, and respecteth not the proud, nor such as turn aside to lies.*

Titus 3:5

Not by works of righteousness which we have done, but according to his mercy he saved us, by the washing of regeneration, and renewing of the Holy Ghost.

Romans 12:1-2

I beseech you therefore, brethren, by the mercies of God, that ye present your bodies a living sacrifice, holy, acceptable unto God, which is your reasonable service. And be not conformed to this world: but be ye transformed by the renewing of your mind, that ye may prove what is that good, and accept-able, and perfect, will of God.

Psalm 60:12

Through God we shall do valiantly: for he it is that shall tread down our enemies.

Psalm 31:14-15

But I trusted in thee, O Lord: I said, Thou art my God. My times are in thy hand: deliver me from the hand of mine enemies, and from them that persecute me.

Job 8:13

So are the paths of all that forget God; and the hypocrite's hope shall perish.

Jeremiah 1:5-19

Before I formed thee in the belly I knew thee; and before thou camest forth out of the womb I sanctified thee, and I ordained thee a prophet unto the nations. Then said I, Ah, LORD GOD! behold, I cannot speak: for I am a child.

But the LORD said unto me, Say not, I am a child: for thou shalt go to all that I shall send thee, and whatsoever I command thee thou shalt speak. Be not afraid of their faces: for I am with thee to deliver thee, saith the LORD.

Then the LORD put forth his hand, and touched my mouth. And the LORD said unto me, Behold, I have put my words in thy mouth.

See, I have this day set thee over the nations and over the kingdoms, to root out, and to pull down, and to destroy, and to throw down, to build, and to plant.

Moreover the word of the LORD came unto me, saying, Jeremiah, what seest thou?

And I said, I see a rod of an almond tree.

Then said the LORD unto me, Thou hast well seen: for I will hasten my word to perform it.

And the word of the LORD came unto me the second time, saying, What seest thou?

And I said, I see a seething pot; and the face thereof is toward the north.

Then the LORD said unto me, Out of the north an evil shall break forth upon all the inhabitants of the land. For, lo, I will call all the families of the kingdoms of the north, saith the LORD; and they shall come, and they shall set every one his throne at the entering of the gates of Jerusalem, and against all the walls thereof round about, and against all the cities of Judah.

And I will utter my judgments against them touching all their wickedness, who have forsaken me, and have burned incense unto other gods, and worshipped the works of their own hands.

Thou therefore gird up thy loins, and arise, and speak unto them all that I command thee: be not dismayed at their faces, lest I confound thee before them. For, behold, I have made thee this day a defenced city, and an iron pillar, and brasen walls against the whole land, against the kings of Judah, against the princes thereof, against the *priests thereof, and against the people of the land. And they shall fight against thee; but they shall not prevail against thee; for I am with thee, saith the LORD, to deliver thee.*

Proverbs 21:20

There is treasure to be desired and oil in the dwelling of the wise; but a foolish man spendeth it up.

Proverbs 3:6

In all thy ways acknowledge him, and he shall direct thy paths.

Proverbs 22:7

The rich ruleth over the poor, and the borrower is servant to the lender.

Proverbs 13:22

A good man leaveth an inheritance to his children's children: and the wealth of the sinner is laid up for the just.

Psalm 59:11

Slay them not, lest my people forget: scatter them by thy power; and bring them down, O LORD our shield.

Psalm 58:11

So that a man shall say, Verily there is a reward for the righteous: verily he is a God that judgeth in the earth.

1 Peter 1:21

Who by him do believe in God, that raised him up from the dead, and gave him glory; that your faith and hope might be in God.

Galatians 5:1

Stand fast therefore in the liberty wherewith Christ hath made us free, and be not entangled again with the yoke of bondage.

Romans 15:13

Now the God of hope fill you with all joy and peace in believing, that ye may abound in hope, through the power of the Holy Ghost.

Leviticus 19:31

Regard not them that have familiar spirits, neither seek after wizards, to be defiled by them: I am the LORD your God.

1 Corinthians 6:19-20

What? know ye not that your body is

the temple of the Holy Ghost which is in you, which ye have of God, and ye are not your own? For ye are bought with a price: therefore glorify God in your body, and in your spirit, which are God's.

Matthew 13:3-9

And he spake many things unto them in parables, saying, Behold, a sower went forth to sow; and when he sowed, some seeds fell by the way side, and the fowls came and devoured them up: Some fell upon stony places, where they had not much earth: and forthwith they sprung up, because they had no deepness of earth: and when the sun was up, they were scorched; and because they had no root, they withered away.

And some fell among thorns; and the thorns sprung up, and choked them: but other fell into good ground, and brought forth fruit, some an hundredfold, some sixtyfold, some thirtyfold.

Isaiah 40:31

But they that wait upon the LORD shall renew their strength; they shall mount up with wings as eagles; they shall run, and not be weary; and they shall walk, and not faint.

Isaiah 26:3-4

Thou wilt keep him in perfect peace, whose mind is stayed on thee: because he trusteth in thee. Trust ye in the LORD for ever: for in the LORD JEHOVAH is everlasting strength.

Genesis 15:6-10, GNT

Abram put his trust in the LORD, and because of this the LORD was pleased with him and accepted him. Then the LORD said to him, "I am the LORD, who led you out of Ur in Babylonia, to give you this land as your own."

But Abram asked, "Sovereign LORD, how can I know that it will be mine?"

He answered, "Bring me a cow, a goat, and a ram, each of them three years old, and a dove and a pigeon."

Abram brought the animals to God, cut them in half, and placed the halves opposite each other in two rows; but he did not cut up the birds.

Galatians 3:6-9

Even as Abraham believed God, and it was accounted to him for righteousness.

Know ye therefore that they which are of faith, the same are the children of Abraham.

And the scripture, foreseeing that God would justify the heathen through faith, preached before the gospel unto Abraham, saying, In thee shall all nations be blessed. So then they which be of faith are blessed with faithful Abraham.

2 Kings 5:13-15, GW

But Naaman's servants went to him and said, "Master, if the prophet had asked you to do some extraordinary act, wouldn't you have done it? Why shouldn't you do as he said: 'Wash and be clean'?" So he went to dip himself in the Jordan River seven times, as the man of God had instructed him.

His skin became healthy again like a little child's skin. Then he and all his men returned to the man of God. Naaman stood in front of Elisha and said, "Now I know that there's no god in the whole world, except the God of Israel. So please accept a present from me."

Psalm 33:4-6, NIV

The words of the LORD are true, and all his works are dependable. The LORD loves what is righteous and just; his constant love fills the earth. The LORD created the heavens by his command, the sun, moon, and stars by his spoken word.

Jeremiah 11:1-5, NIV

The LORD said to me, "Listen to the

terms of the covenant. Tell the people of Judah and of Jerusalem that I, the LORD God of Israel, have placed a curse on everyone who does not obey the terms of this covenant. It is the covenant I made with their ancestors when I brought them out of Egypt, the land that was like a blazing furnace to them. I told them to obey me and to do everything that I had commanded. I told them that if they obeyed, they would be my people and I would be their God.

"Then I would keep the promise I made to their ancestors that I would give them the rich and fertile land which they now have."

I said, "Yes, LORD."

1 Peter 2:1-5, NIV

Rid yourselves, then, of all evil; no more lying or hypocrisy or jealousy or insulting language. Be like newborn babies, always thirsty for the pure spiritual milk, so that by drinking it you may grow up and be saved.

As the scripture says, "You have found out for yourselves how kind the Lord is." Come to the Lord, the living stone rejected by people as worthless but chosen by God as valuable. Come as living stones, and let yourselves be used in building the spiritual temple, where you will serve as holy priests to offer spiritual and acceptable sacrifices to God through Jesus Christ.

Zechariah 4:6-7, NIV

The angel told me to give Zerubbabel

this message from the LORD: You will succeed, not by military might or by your own strength, but by my spirit. Obstacles as great as mountains will disappear before you. You will rebuild the Temple, and as you put the last stone in place, the people will shout, "Beautiful, beautiful."

1 Corinthians 1:25-26, NIV

For what seems to be God's foolishness is wiser than human wisdom, and what seems to be God's weakness is stronger than human strength. Now remember what you were, my friends, when God called you. From the human point of view few of you were wise or powerful or of high social standing.

Nehemiah 8:10, NIV

Now go home and have a feast. Share your food and wine with those who don't have enough. Today is holy to our LORD, so don't be sad. The joy that the LORD gives you will make you strong.

1 Peter 4:11-12, GNT

Those who preach must preach God's messages; those who serve must serve with the strength that God gives them, so that in all things praise may be given to God through Jesus Christ, to whom belong glory and power forever and ever. Amen.

My dear friends, do not be surprised at the painful test you are suffering, as though something unusual were happening to you.

1 Chronicles 16:11-12

Seek the LORD and his strength, seek his face continually. Remember his marvellous works that he hath done, his wonders, and the judgments of his mouth

Exodus 15:2, GW

The LORD is my strong defender; he is the one who has saved me. He is my God, and I will praise him, my father's God, and I will sing about his greatness.

Isaiah 41:10, GW

Don't be afraid, because I am with you. Don't be intimidated; I am your God. I will strengthen you. I will help you. I will support you with my victorious right hand.

Isaiah 40:28-31, NIV

Do you not know? Have you not heard? The LORD is the everlasting God, the Creator of the ends of the earth. He will not grow tired or weary, and his understanding no one can fathom.

He gives strength to the weary and increases the power of the weak. Even youths grow tired and weary, and young men stumble and fall; but those who hope in the LORD will renew their strength. They will soar on wings like eagles; they will run and not grow weary, they will walk and not be faint.

Psalm 29:11, NIV

The LORD gives strength to his people; the LORD blesses his people with peace.

John 14:27

Peace I leave with you, my peace I give unto you: not as the world giveth, give I unto you. Let not your heart be troubled, neither let it be afraid.

Psalm 55:22

Cast thy burden upon the LORD, and he shall sustain thee: he shall never suffer the righteous to be moved.

Psalm 37:39-40

But the salvation of the righteous is of the LORD: he is their strength in the time of trouble. And the LORD shall help them, and deliver them: he shall deliver them from the wicked, and save them, because they trust in him.

Psalm 37:25-26

I have been young, and now am old; yet have I not seen the righteous forsaken, nor his seed begging bread. He is ever merciful, and lendeth; and his seed is blessed.

Psalm 37:18-19, GW

The LORD knows the daily struggles of innocent people. Their inheritance will last forever. They will not be put to shame in trying times. Even in times of famine they will be satisfied.

Psalm 37:16-17

The LORD knoweth the days of the up-right: and their inheritance shall be for ever. They shall not be ashamed in the evil time: and in the days of famine they shall be satisfied.

Psalm 37:10-11

For yet a little while, and the wicked shall not be: yea, thou shalt diligently consider his place, and it shall not be. But the meek shall inherit the earth; and shall delight themselves in the abundance of peace.

Psalm 37:7-8

*Rest in the L*ORD*, and wait patiently for him: fret not thyself because of him who prospereth in his way, because of the man who bringeth wicked devices to pass. Cease from anger, and forsake wrath: fret not thyself in any wise to do evil.*

Psalm 37:5

*Commit thy way unto the L*ORD*; trust also in him; and he shall bring it to pass.*

Psalm 36:5-9, NIV

Your love, O LORD, reaches to the heavens, your faithfulness to the skies. Your righteousness is like the mighty mountains, your justice like the great deep.

O LORD, you preserve both man and beast. How priceless is your unfailing love! Both high and low among men find refuge in the shadow of your wings. They feast on the abundance of your house; you give them drink from your river of delights. For with you is the fountain of life; in your light we see light.

Luke 16:10

He that is faithful in that which is least is faithful also in much: and he that is unjust in the least is unjust also in much.

Psalm 56:4 NIV

In God, whose word I praise, in God I trust; I will not be afraid. What can mortal man do to me?

Psalm 27:13

I had fainted, unless I had believed to see the goodness of the LORD in the land of the living.

Other Books
by
Prophetess Jackie Harewood

The Violent Take It by Force

Intercession Builds Bridges: Frequently Asked Questions About Intercession

Overshadowed by the Almighty

Ballistic Apostolic Prayer

Using Your Most Powerful Weapon

Make A Joyful Noise: An Introduction to Praise and Worship

The Violent Take it by Force

Intercession Made Eas

Jackie Harewood

Overshadowed

by the Almighty

Understanding
the Phenomenon
Known as
"Being Slain
in the Spirit"

With a special
chapter entitled
What Does God's Voice
Sound Like?

Prophetess Jackie Harewood

Ballistic Apostolic Prayer

Jackie Harewood

Learning

to

Use

Your

Greatest

Weapon

Prophetess Jackie Harewood

MAKE A JOYFUL NOISE

An Introduction to Praise and Worship

**Prophetess
Jackie
Harewood**

I *Will* Bless THEE

Discovering the Untapped Power of COVENANT

Apostle David Harewood

AUTHOR CONTACT PAGE

Prophetess Jackie Harewood
37041 Agnes Webb Avenue
Prairieville, LA 70769

(225) 772-4552

www.fcimbr.wordpress.com
www.iffcm.wordpress.com

jharewoodla@icloud.com

www.ingramcontent.com/pod-product-compliance
Lightning Source LLC
LaVergne TN
LVHW011158080426
835508LV00007B/473